# GROWING
# AND USING
# HERBS

# ALAN TITCHMARSH

# GROWING AND USING
# HERBS

HAMLYN

## Acknowledgements

*Cover photograph by Photos Horticultural*
*Title page photograph copyright BBC Enterprises*
*Line artwork by Marilyn Day*

*Photographs*
Pat Brindley, pages 10, 15, 23, 24, 40, 43, 51, 54; The Iris
Hardwick Library, pages 20, 34; Jerry Harpur, pages 18–19;
The Mansell Collection (London), pages 14, 41; Tania
Midgley, 24, 49; Photographie Giraudon (Paris), pages 12–13;
Photos Horticultural, pages 17, 37; The Harry Smith
Horticultural Photographic Collection, pages 26, 42.

This book is based on *Herbs* first published in 1984
by The Hamlyn Publishing Group Limited.

This revised edition published in 1986 by Hamlyn Publishing,
Bridge House, London Road, Twickenham, Middlesex, England

ISBN 0 600 30709 3

Phototypeset in England by Servis Filmsetting Limited
in 10 on 11pt Apollo

Printed in Spain by Cayfosa. Barcelona
Dep. Leg. B-11518-1986

# CONTENTS

Mint does not have to be plain green but even this decorative variegated form is extremely vigorous

# INTRODUCTION

Small gardens have distinct advantages: they grow to maturity quickly; they are relatively easy to maintain, and they can be planted up with only a modest amount of expense. The one disadvantage they have is that they will contain only a limited number of plants, which means that every single occupant has to earn its keep. This is where herbs come into their own.

Until a couple of years ago I'd grown just a handful of herbs mixed in with my border plants. They weren't too far away from the back door, which is handy on those wet days when you don't want to trudge half a mile for a sprig of mint for the pan of peas. But then I decided I wanted a proper herb garden; not a large one, but one which was formal with two small borders divided by a central brick and gravel path. It's only 3m wide and 8m long (about 10ft by 27ft) but it has given tremendous pleasure in the short time it's been establishing itself.

In the centre of the path, just half way down the plot, is a brick circle around which stand four terra-cotta rhubarb pots. Thyme and pennyroyal and chamomile spill over the path at intervals and mix with the lovage and hyssop, lavender and chives and all the rest of the fragrant goodies that make up the border furniture. Four gooseberry bushes give a bit of shrubby height, and at one end is a chamomile seat on which the tired visitor can take fragrant repose after a summer walk.

All this sounds expensive. But it's not. All the herbs that could be were raised from seed. Fifty of more plants of rue or marjoram or thyme cost me only a few pence if you don't count the cost of a seed tray and a bit of compost. Odd specialities that couldn't be raised from seeds were bought very cheaply at a local agricultural show, and so my elegant garden cost me very little.

All of which cheers me up considerably on a balmy summer's day when I can quickly splash a hosepipe over the herb border to help them release their fragrances while I recline on my chamomile-cushioned seat. Now that is real living!

# HERBS IN HISTORY

For flavouring soup, for weaving a magic spell or for killing off a deadly enemy, herbs have always been useful to man, and although the term 'herb' can be applied to any plant that dies down to the ground in winter, to most folk a herb is a plant that's used in the kitchen.

Herbs today might be thought of as a luxury, but before the discovery of modern drugs they were the living medicine chest attached to every house. There were herbs to sooth fevers, herbs to keep you regular, herbs to cure rashes, and a few to send the goblins scurrying away in terror.

Not all cures worked with great efficiency, but some of them did, and homoeopathy continues to thrive, using countless preparations based on herbs.

Chives and garlic are said to help prevent blackspot of roses when they are planted around rose beds.

# HERBS IN HISTORY

When smells in the city became as much of a problem as disease, the fragrance of herbs came into its own. Nosegays held close to the face presented a more pleasing perfume than open drains, and the arrangement of herbs in formal patterns within the garden, enabled them to be grown for ornament as well as health.

But it is in flavouring food that today's gardener finds herbs most useful. The Romans enjoyed spiced-up fare, too, and introduced many herbs to Britain. Many were lost during the Dark Ages, but returned during the Norman Conquests and have been with us ever since, livening up dishes that would otherwise be bland and boring. So be adventurous – don't stick to parsley and mint; try something new the next time you cook a Sunday lunch!

This 16th century tapestry shows the geometric form many early herb gardens took

# Herbs in the Garden

There's absolutely no reason why you shouldn't spread your herbs all over the garden, but it does mean that you've got to remember just where each one is when you want a snippet for an omelette or a sprig for a salad. It's more convenient, and more fun, too, if you can grow them all in one place where their perfume will fill the air on warm summer days.

Nearly all herbs relish brilliant sunshine. Many of them come from warm countries and need sun to bring out their flavour as well as their aroma. Planted around a patio they'll enjoy life to the full, and you'll have the double pleasure of finding them easy to pick and pleasant to sit near.

Bear in mind the height and spread of each herb (as well as it's form and colour) before deciding on its planting position. Some herbs are rampant and will swamp more delicate treasures. Plants like mint and lemon balm are rampageous. Plant them in bottomless buckets which can be sunk into the ground with their rims protruding. With any luck you'll be able to prevent their questing roots from exploring too far.

A 16th century woodcut of a raised herb bed

Build a raised brick 'box' just 45cm (1½ft) high; fill it with soil and plant it up with chamomile to make a fragrant seat.

Spring is the best time to plant, though the fact that herbs can be bought in pots means that planting is possible at any time of year, provided that the soil's not dust dry or frozen solid.

Any reasonable soil will suit them. Don't go overboard on the manure; most herbs don't need it and will grow best in soil that's been dug or forked over and given just a sprinkling of fertiliser such as blood, bone and fishmeal. Too rich a soil will make herbs sappy and gross. In soil that's really poor and sandy, garden compost, peat or leafmould is helpful in holding moisture and bulking up the soil. Work it in a few weeks before planting.

## Herbs for shade

If you simply don't possess a sunny spot there are just a few herbs that will grow in shade. Try these:

- Angelica
- Chervil
- Chives
- Lovage
- Mint
- Parsley

Stepping stones make herb gathering more convenient

## Finding herbs

Most local nurseries and garden centres nowadays sell a good range of herbs in pots, but the best selection is offered by specialist nurseries. Buy in person if you can; it's more fun to choose the plants you want rather than to rely on them being chosen and sent through the post. Mind you, most mail order nurseries have a high standard of quality and you'll seldom be disappointed with the results, provided you give the plants a good start.

Water the plants an hour or two before they are to be planted. Remove their pots at planting time and, after digging a hole for the roots with a trowel, lower the plant in and firm back the earth really well. Don't plant too deeply – the 'crown' of the plant (where shoots meet roots) should be just below the surface of the soil. Herbs hate being buried too deeply, but they won't enjoy life if half their roots are above ground level.

Water the plants in thoroughly and don't let them dry out during their first year, otherwise they'll not establish a hefty root system that will lead to healthy growth in the future.

I've shown the height and spread of each herb in the A to Z sections on pages 25 to 55 to give you some idea of how far apart to set the plants.

## Herbs in pots

Most herbs will grow a treat in pots, provided they can sink their roots into some reasonable compost and are well supplied with water and light.

They will never do well indoors. Herbs are hardy plants and simply grow tall and spindly in the heat and comparative gloom of a living room. Have a potful of basil by the sink if you want, but don't expect it to thrive for long.

If the pots can be stored on an outside windowsill the herbs will be fine. Here they'll receive plenty of light and fresh air which will result in good growth. They love to grow on balconies and roof gardens, too, so long as gales don't blow them away.

Young herb plants can generally be put into larger pots

Herbs in terra-cotta pots arranged to create a formal garden of a different type and suitable for any bright patio

as soon as they are bought in spring. Plastic or clay pots 13cm (5in) in diameter are suitable, and will usually fit comfortably on an outside windowsill. Use John Innes No.2 potting compost, or a mixture of this and a peat-based compost such as Levington or Arthur Bowers. Peat-based compost alone tends to shrink when dry and herbs in pots are very quick to dry out.

Use the same compost mixture when herbs are being grown in window boxes, but whatever the container,

Wear a sprig of rue in your hair when weeding in summer; it's supposed to ward off flies!

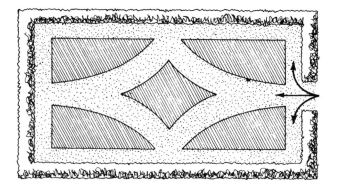

A simple design for a formal herb garden

*Right:* The white statue forms a striking focal point in this herb garden at Jenkyn Place. Note, too, the plants growing through gaps in the paving – an attractive and aromatic feature

Brighten up your salads with flower petals. Use the blooms of pot marigolds, pansies, polyanthuses, bergamot, hyssop and nasturtiums – they're all edible.

make sure that it has plenty of drainage holes to allow excess water to escape. Badly drained containers will turn into muddy ponds in winter and herbs are notoriously bad swimmers.

As they grow the plants can be given larger pots. Spring is the best time for repotting. Use the same compost mixture as before and choose a pot that is 5cm (2in) larger in diamter. Old and tired herbs can be discarded in favour of young and healthy ones which can be bought or raised from seeds and cuttings (see page 22).

## Patterns with herbs

The fact that they were once used in formal gardens and grown in intricate patterns has led herbs to be planted in

A traditional knot garden planted with herbs

all sorts of odd ways; some of which are mentioned below.

Old cartwheels can be painted and laid flat on the ground over prepared soil, and a different herb planted in each space between the spokes. If a long, narrow bed will fit more neatly into your plot than a circular one, use an old ladder instead of a cartwheel.

But it's more fun, and much more original, to make a formal garden to your own design using paving slabs or bricks and patches of herbs. There are countless patterns to be stitched with herbs and stonework to make a fragrant patchwork tapestry. All you need to do is bear in mind the relative heights and colours of your neighbouring herbs.

# Harvesting and Storing

Most herbs reach their peak of flavour just before they flower, and if they have to be stored for winter use, that's the time to gather them. Snip off suitable stems early in the day (taking them from all over the plant to leave it looking shapely) and dry them as quickly as possible. I know it looks pretty to have bunches of herbs hanging in the kitchen, but most.of the flavour will be lost. Herbs need to be dried in a dark place, and the best bet is really a cool oven or an airing cupboard.

As soon as the leaves are crisp, strip them from the stems and crush them. To seal in flavour they should be stored in airtight containers that do not admit light. If they have to go in transparent jars, keep the jars in a dark cupboard. They'll store for at least a year. Herbs that dry well include:

- Rosemary
- Fennel
- Basil
- Lemon Balm
- Sage
- Bay

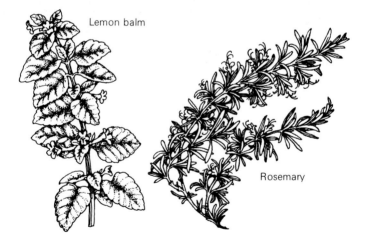

Lemon balm

Rosemary

Some herbs lose their flavour when dried and are better frozen. Wash the sprigs, dry them by patting with kitchen roll, then place them in polythene bags and put

French marigolds planted among tomatoes will sometimes help to keep whitefly at bay.

them straight in the freezer. They'll lose their shape when thawed but not much of their flavour. These are all recommended for freezing:

- Marjoram
- Parsley
- Chervil
- Tarragon
- Mint
- Lovage
- Chives
- Dill
- Fennel
- Basil

Chives            Lovage

## MAKING MORE HERBS

I will mention how each herb can be propagated in the A to Z of Culinary Herbs, but it's worth giving just a few brief details of each method.

Seeds are easy to sow – simply fork over the patch of soil where they are to grow, lightly rake it level, scatter the seeds thinly over the surface and lightly rake again. Never let the soil dry out before the plants are well established. If the seedlings are crowded together, tnin them out to leave one every 10cm (4in) or so. Wider spacings will be necessary for larger plants.

Division of large clumps can be carried out in spring or autumn, as a rule. Dig up the clump and pull it apart into fist-sized pieces which can be replanted at suitable spacings. Dead sections can be thrown away and any spares given to friends.

Cuttings of shoot tips are taken in summer and usually root quickest in a pot of seed and cuttings compost on a windowsill.

Cuttings of most herbs should be about 8cm (3in) long and sliced cleanly below a leaf joint at the base. Remove all the lower leaves before inserting the cuttings around the edge of the pot.

Extra humidity is always appreciated at this time and a polythene bag can be placed over the pot. Don't let the cuttings burn up in full sun.

## Herb care

Don't forget that herbs are garden plants that need kindness, just like the brilliant bloomers in your summer bedding. Occasional feeds with liquid fertiliser will be beneficial in summer (two or three times between April and September will do them nicely).

Left to their own devices, many herbs become straggly. Clip them over with a pair of shears in spring if they make dense bushes, or pinch out the growing shoot tips if the stems are more sparse. Herbaceous herbs that die down in winter should have all their dead stems removed.

The golden form of lemon balm – see page 33

Put sprigs of mint on your cabbages in the garden to help repel those voracious cabbage white caterpillars.

Fennel, with its tall stature and feathery foliage makes an ideal background planting for a small garden

Use one plant of fennel as a focal point in gardens too small for large shrubs or trees – the fennel provides stature without outgrowing its welcome.

# A to Z of Culinary Herbs

It's in the very nature of herbs that they can be used in the kitchen, but the following list includes only those plants which are most popularly added to gastronomic delights. Those that are nearly always grown because they look pretty (and which most folk are unsure how to use) will be found on pages 41 to 55.

## Angelica *(Angelica archangelica)*

One of the stateliest and most statuesque herbs you'll ever grow. The sturdy hollow flower stalk pushes up in the second year of the plant's life to a height of around 2.5m (8ft) and opens its white flowers on umbrella spokes in summer. The leaves are bold yet ferny, and a refreshing shade of green. Give the plant room to grow; it will spread 1 to 1.25m (3 to 4ft) across. As it is a biennial it should be sown afresh each year, to flower at the age of two.

Angelica is one of those rare herbs that prefers to grow in semi-shade. Sow the seeds in April or September in the soil where the plants are to grow.

Cut the flower stems for crystallizing in May or June, before the flowers are properly developed. Fresh leaves can be added to preserves, fruit compotes and cold drinks. Pieces of crystallized stem are used as decoration for cakes. The leaves can also be used to make tea, though it hardly ranks with Earl Gray when it comes to flavour.

## Basil *(Ocimum basilicum)*

Basil is an annual, so however well you grow it you'll have to raise new plants from seed each spring. Scatter a few seeds in a pot of seed compost, cover them lightly with more compost and germinate them on the kitchen windowsill or in a warm, dark cupboard. When the seedlings are large enough to be handled they can be pricked out at the rate of one to an 8-cm (3-in) pot. Plant them in a sunny spot in the garden or in a pot stood outside in late May when danger of frost is past. Pinching out the shoot tips occasionally will help to keep them bushy. The leaves are glossy and green (or rich purple in the variety 'Dark Opal') and the flowers small and white.

Basil will grow about 45cm (1½ft) high and wide, and fresh leaves can be gathered as soon as the plant is large enough. In late summer more leaves can be harvested and

A statuesque angelica plant dominates this herb border

Rub the leaves of summer savoury on bee stings for relief.

dried for winter use. Leaves also retain their flavour when frozen – those that are dried gradually become less flavoursome.

On buttered carrots and sliced tomatoes basil is a knock-out! It's also recommended for salads, soups and sauces, all kinds of meat, poultry and game, fish, cheese and pasta.

## Bay *(Laurus nobilis)*

A bay bush in the garden will save you pounds over the years. It's an evergreen shrub and can be allowed to grow unrestricted or else clipped into lollipop or pyramidal shapes during summer. It's not as hard as nails, so find it a sunny and sheltered spot in well-drained soil. Better still, grow it in a tub that can be taken into a frost-free greenhouse in winter. If tub-grown plants have to stay outdoors in winter, wrap sacking or straw around the container to offer a little insulation to the roots.

Plant bay trees in spring. Cuttings are difficult to root, so young plants are the best bet. Leave a bay tree to grow and it will reach 15m (50ft) and more, but it's easy to restrict by summer pruning – use the clippings in the kitchen.

Searing winter winds will cause leaf browning. Pick the fresh leaves at any time of year. Dry them in summer for winter use by friends. One leaf will flavour an entire meal.

Bay

## Borage *(Borago officinalis)*

Borage must be the easiest herb to grow. Scatter the seeds over a patch of sunny, well-drained soil in spring or autumn and plants will emerge every year thereafter. The leaves and stems are densely hairy and the nodding flowers are blue stars that shine all summer. Each plant will grow 60cm (2ft) high and as much across.

The flowers make a pretty garnish to fruit cups like Pimms, and the young leaves can be chopped and added to cheese or yoghurt, or else fried in pancake batter.

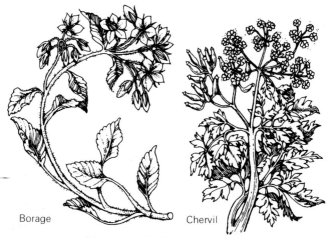

Borage                                                           Chervil

## Caraway *(Carum carvi)*

It's the seeds of caraway that are used for flavouring. Sow them in late summer on a patch of sunny, well-drained soil where the plant is to grow and they'll be produced again at the end of the following year. Caraway is grown as a biennial and sown afresh each September.

The leaves look like finely cut parsley and the flowers like cow parsley, on a plant that is 60cm (2ft) high and 30cm (1ft) across.

Cut the stems just before the seeds are ripe and hang them up in paper bags so that all the seeds are caught. They are the traditional ingredient of seed cakes, and can also be added to cheese, cabbage, goulash and bread.

Herbs certainly pay their way; they are attractive, most smell delightful and they are useful in the kitchen

## Chervil *(Anthriscus cerefolium)*

Chervil looks even more like cow parsley than caraway and grows to around 45cm (1½ft) high and 30cm (1ft) wide. Grow the plant as an annual, sowing the seeds on the soil where they are to grow in spring, and thinning out the seedlings while they are quite small. Dappled shade and a moisture-retentive soil are enjoyed.

The flavour is one of mild aniseed and the fresh leaves can be used during summer. Chop off the flowerheads. Chervil dries badly but can be frozen. It's a classic ingredient of 'fines herbes' and can be used to flavour all manner of dishes such as salads, game, omelettes, soups and sauces, eggs, cream cheese, fish and meat. It's a good garnish, too.

## Chives *(Allium schoenoprasum)*

The daintiest of the onions, chives makes upright tufts of bright green leaves that are decorated with lilac-pink pom-pon flowers in summer. Cut the blooms off if you want the plant to retain all its flavour. It will grow about 23cm (9in) high and spreads to make a tidy clump in sun

---

Dried and powdered leaves of pennyroyal are often recommended for sprinkling around doors and windows to repel ants.

The spikey foliage of chives has a mild onion flavour and the pompon flowers make this plant a real garden asset

or dappled shade. Divide clumps in spring or autumn to make more plants or keep existing ones in check.

Chives enjoys any decent soil and benefits from having its faded foliage chopped off in spring. The leaves can be used fresh from early to late summer, and frozen for winter use. Their mild onion flavour perks up boiled eggs, cream cheese, soups and salads, fish, meat and poultry.

## Coriander *(Coriandrum sativum)*

Often used but seldom grown, coriander is another of those herbs belonging to the parsley family, so its leaves are finely cut and its white or pale lilac flowers carried on

Make a formal herb garden by planting the herbs within a geometric pattern composed of clipped box, cotton lavender (santolina) and lavender.

umbrella-like heads. It's an annual, grows 45cm (1½ft) high and 30cm (1ft) across, and should be sown outdoors where it is to grow in spring. Well-drained soil and sun are essential. The fresh leaves can be cut in summer and used in curries and pickles, but it's the seeds that are most prized.

The plant will smell thoroughly unpleasant until the seeds ripen, then its full aroma is released. Gather the stalks and put them in bags to catch the ripening seeds. Use them to flavour ratatouille, soups and sauces, fish, meat, poultry, duck and game.

## Dill *(Anethum graveolens)*

Like a miniature fennel at first glance, dill makes a feathery plant up to 60cm (2ft) or so high and has clusters of yellow flowers at the stem tips. It's an annual and needs to be sown afresh where it is to grow each spring, and though it enjoys a well-drained soil and sun, it isn't very happy in drought.

Fresh leaves can be cut and used as soon as the plants are large enough to rob; seeds are collected from the flowerheads just before they are shed naturally. Tie bunches of flower stalks in paper bags to catch your bounty. The leaves can be frozen, too.

Seeds are used in dill vinegar, pickles, bread and biscuits. Fresh leaves can be used in salads, cooked vegetables and egg dishes, as well as casseroles.

Dill

Beware the following herbs if your garden is small: borage, lemon balm, mint, tansy, horseradish, comfrey. They'll all try to make a takeover bid.

Fennel

### Fennel *(Foeniculum vulgare)*

This graceful, feathery monster is a back-of-the-border plant in most gardens, but if you bring it forward within touching distance you'll be able to enjoy at close quarters the aniseed-scented filigree foliage. It grows a good 1.5m (5ft) high, and is best in its purple-leaved form, on which the acid-yellow flowers contrast well. It needs sun and well-drained soil and is perennial – once you've planted it it will stick around. Established clumps can be divided in spring; new plants can be raised from seed sown outdoors in spring.

Leaves can be used fresh in summer or frozen or dried. Stems are used in Provençale dishes. Leaves are good with sauces and soups, salads and stuffings, and with fish, lamb and pork.

### Garlic *(Allium sativum)*

Garlic is a herb for gamblers (it needs a good summer) but it costs very little to buy a bulb in spring, split it into cloves and plant these 10cm (4in) apart as for onion sets. The soil should be well cultivated and sharply drained, and by autumn plump bulbs should be ready for harvesting. Lift the bulbs and store them in a cool, dry, well-lit place once the leaves have started to turn yellow.

Use garlic in anything you like!

### Horseradish *(Cochlearia armoracia)*

Plant this once and you'll never lose it. Large, green, dock-like leaves push up through the soil for quite a long way around, and will eventually give rise to 1.25-m (4-ft) stalks of white flowers in summer. It's really best restricted in a sunken enclosure of slates or tiles. It enjoys sun and a rich, moist soil. Pieces of the thick root can be planted in spring, and these form the best means of propagation.

It's the thick tap root that's used to make horseradish sauce, and it can be harvested at any time of year.

## Lemon balm *(Melissa officinalis)*

Don't be fooled by that deceptively gentle name; balm is as rampant as mint. Grow it in a sunken bucket or similar enclosure to prevent it from swamping other plants. It's a perennial that will grow 60cm (2ft) high and even wider, and it is best in its golden form 'Aurea' and just as flavoursome. Its rough, oval leaves smell deliciously of lemons when crushed. The flowers are insignificant.

Plant balm in autumn or spring in any reasonable soil in sun or light shade. It is definitely perennial and divides easily in spring or autumn. Use fresh leaves in summer; dry or freeze them for winter. Good with fish, poultry, meat and salads. Crystallize the leaves for desserts.

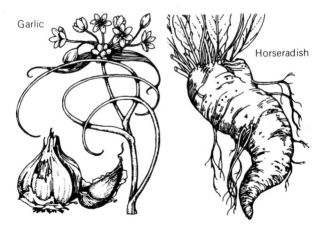

Garlic

Horseradish

The dried leaves of costmary, or alecost, make very good bookmarks.

Herbs in flower display a subtle range of colours

## Lovage *(Ligusticum officinale)*

Leaves like celery and umbrella-like flowers of pale green on towering stems give lovage a unique appearance. It grows to a stunning 2.5m (8ft) high, and 1.25m (4ft)

Scatter the seeds of thyme in the crevices among paving stones in early spring. The germinating plants will survive the occasional trampling and scent the air at each footfall.

across so needs plenty of room to stretch itself. Seeds sown in spring will produce flowering plants in the second year, and these will survive for a number of seasons. Rich soil in dappled shade is most enjoyed by this plant.

Mature plants can be divided in spring and the divisions replanted. Mind you, you'll not want many of these! Gather the leaves for use during the growing season. They freeze and dry well, too, retaining their zingy celery flavour. Use them in soups and stews and on salads. The seeds can be used for decorating bread and biscuits.

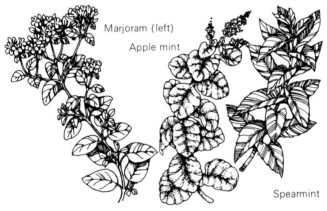

Marjoram (left)

Apple mint

Spearmint

## Marjoram *(Origanum onites)*

Pot marjoram is a popular and easily accommodated herb with an appetizing aroma. It grows to around 30cm (1ft) high and rather more across and produces neat flower clusters that are usually pink; sometimes white. The leaves are small and rather downy.

Give marjoram a spot in full sun and a well-drained soil. Seeds can be sown where the plant is required to grow in spring, or mature clumps can be divided, also in spring. It's a perennial.

Harvest the leaves just before the plant flowers for maximum flavour. They freeze well. It's a versatile herb that's used in stews, soups and sauces, and with all manner of meats and vegetables. Try it and see.

## Mint *(Mentha* species*)*

There are dozens of mints, scented of anything from Eau de Cologne to pineapple (though you'll have to use your imagination with some of them). They are all invasive and need to be grown in a sunken bottomless bucket or tin bath to prevent them from roaming too far. Division is the easiest form of propagation and can be carried out in autumn or spring.

Give mint a rich soil if you can; it will put up with sun or dappled shade but it doesn't enjoy drought. The purple flower spikes carried on stems up to 75cm (2½ft) high are a grand sight in summer.

Use fresh leaves whenever they are around to pick. They dry or freeze well and make delicious sauce for lamb. Try them also in savoury butter, as a garnish in fruit cups or crystallized.

## Parsley *(Petroselinum crispum)*

The frilly and crispy leaves of parsley hardly need to be described, but do remember that the herb is best sown afresh each year. Too many gardeners try to keep a clump going for ever. It's a neat plant, growing about 15cm (6in) high and it makes a good edging to flower beds and vegetable patches.

Sow the seeds where they are to grow in spring. Be patient; they take ages to germinate but an overnight soak in water before sowing will hurry them up. Find a spot in sun or dappled shade. The plant is a biennial and will gradually become delapidated in its second year. Gather fresh all the year round if you can protect a few plants with cloches; otherwise freeze some leaves for winter use. Add the leaves to whatever you like, especially parsley sauce, Maître d'Hôtel butter and bouquet garni. The leaves are the classic garnish used in pubs and restaurants.

## Rosemary *(Rosmarinus officinalis)*

Although it suffers in really severe winters, rosemary will usually come through unscathed to continue pushing upwards its spire-like stems, thickly clothed in

---

Dig up a clump of mint in late summer and plant it in a pot. Kept in a cool, bright place indoors it will carry on producing flavoursome leaves during the winter.

narrow, dark green leaves that are sweetly savoury. It is evergreen and a valuable backbone shrub in any sunny, well-drained border, and with any luck its pale lavender flowers will decorate the stems every spring. It usually grows to around 1.25m (4ft) and as much across, but in spots where it is happy it may be even taller.

Cuttings of firm shoot tips will root in a pot or outdoors from mid- to late summer. Leave them for a year before transplanting them.

Use fresh leaves all the year round in sauces and soups, with lamb, chicken and pork and in stuffings.

## Sage *(Salvia officinalis)*

The coloured-leaved cultivars of sage such as 'Icterina', yellow and green; 'Tricolor', pink, purple and cream; and

Variegated- and purple-leaved cultivars of sage

Parsley is supposed to take a long time to germinate because it goes nine times to the devil before it emerges. It always grows best in rich soil.

'Purpurea', soft mauve, are just as good in the kitchen as the plain green form, and even more decorative in the garden. The leaves of all are attractively felted, and the plants make neat hummocks around 45cm (18in) high and even more across. Plant them in well-drained soil in a sunny spot, and propagate them from stem tip cuttings in summer – they will root easily in a pot of compost covered with a polythene bag and stood on a windowsill. Clip back the shoots of old and tatty plants in spring.

Harvest fresh nearly all the year round, but the offerings are meagre in winter so dry or freeze some summer leaves. A traditional ingredient of stuffings; good, too, in soups and sauces, with pork and poultry.

## Sorrel *(Rumex acetosa)*

Vinegar leaves, we called them as kids. Rather like a miniature dock in appearance, with arrowhead leaves and spikes of green summer flowers, sorrel will grow to around 30cm (1ft) and maybe 15cm (6in) across. Any ordinary soil, and a spot in full sun or the lightest shade will keep it happy. It's a perennial and can be divided for propagation purposes in spring or autumn, or seeds can be sown where the plants are to grow in spring.

Use the leaves fresh as soon as the plant is large enough to withstand defoliation. Dry or freeze them in summer for winter use. Leaves can be cooked in soups and sauces, and used to flavour salads and vegetables.

## Tarragon *(Artemisia dracunculus)*

It's the French tarragon, rather than the Russian, which has the best flavour. It's a perennial with narrow green leaves on stems around 60cm (2ft) high, and it needs a sunny, sheltered spot, preferably at the foot of a south- or west-facing wall. Cover it with straw or bracken when it dies down in winter. Make sure the soil is well drained. Divide mature clumps to make more plants in spring.

Harvest fresh in summer, and freeze a few leaves at the same time. Use to make tarragon vinegar, and to flavour salad dressings and mustard, butter and sauces, as well as with eggs, fish, meat and poultry. Fresh, chopped leaves can be used as a garnish on salads.

Tarragon  Winter savoury

## Thyme *(Thymus* species*)*

As with mint, there are various flavours of thyme, from
the traditional savoury kind to the lemon-scented ones.
All are small and spreading perennial shrubs with tiny,
aromatic evergreen leaves. They'll make clumps up to
23cm (9in) or so high and three times as much across.
They adore sun and any well-drained soil, and their
flowers of pinkish mauve add greatly to their attraction.
Clip over and divide mature clumps in spring, or sow
seeds at the same time where the plants are to grow.

Use the leaves fresh all the year round, though their
flavour is at its height just before flowering. Dry or freeze
some stems for winter use. Vital in bouquet garni; in
stuffings and sauces. Use with poultry, game, fish and
meat, salads and cooked vegetables.

## Winter savoury *(Satureja montana)*

A neat little shrub with narrow, dark, evergreen leaves.
It grows 30cm (1ft) high and about 45cm (1½ft) across.
Bright sunshine and a well-drained soil are essential. Sow
the seeds where they are to grow in spring, or divide
mature clumps at the same time. Protection with a cloche
or straw will help the plant through the winter in the
north and in exposed situations.

Harvest fresh sprigs all the year round. Use as for sage
and on all manner of cooked vegetables.

---

In the 17th century soup made from thyme and beer was
thought to help overcome shyness. How much of its efficacy
was due to the thyme is not clear.

*Monarda didyma* or bergamot can be easily increased by division and is available in a range of flower colours

# A to Z of Ornamental Herbs

Although herbalists would refute the assertion that any herb should be purely ornamental, I retain my devout cowardice and lack of adventure where many of them are concerned, preferring to grow them simply because of their looks and pleasant smell, rather than for any culinary or medicinal benefits they may offer. These are they; you can experiment if you wish!

## Bergamot (*Monarda didyma*)

Also known as bee balm because bees love the whorls of dragon-mouth flowers that open in summer.

'Cambridge Scarlet', with deep rosy red flowers, strikes me as being far more robust than the purple or pink varieties offered. It's a plant for a sunny spot but it does enjoy a moisture retentive soil in preference to one that bakes in summer. The plant grows 60cm (2ft) or so high and rather more across and its oval leaves smell just like Earl Grey tea. It does not, however, produce the genuine oil of bergamot – that's a distinction that belongs to a variety of citrus fruit.

In the days when sugar was scarce bergamot was grown near hives to attract the bees, hence its nickname of bee balm

Try growing bergamot alongside the garden pool; it will thrive in the damp soil at the water's edge.

The flowerless form of chamomile is suitable for planting a small lawn or a fragrant seat

Buy one plant; settle it into the moist soil and it will soon multiply and allow you to propagate it by division in autumn or spring.

Even the most unadventurous gardener can risk using the leaves and flowers of bergamot in pot-pourri, and the chopped leaves or flowers will pep up the salads of more enterprising cooks.

## Chamomile (*Anthemis nobilis*)

A bright green and fluffy plant that spreads across the ground with runners after the fashion of a strawberry. Walk on these fragile looking but amazingly robust rosettes and they'll emit a deeply fruity fragrance. The flowerless form 'Treneague' is the best one to use for chamomile lawns, plant rooted cuttings at 23cm (9in) intervals; while the double-flowered form is the most ornamental.

All can be planted in spring and propagation is quick and easy by dibbing in severed rosettes. Any ordinary and well-drained soil suits chamomile.

Peter Rabbit had to suffer chamomile tea at bedtime instead of bread and milk and blackberries, so Beatrix

Potter at least considered the latter preferable when it comes to flavour. The dried flowers can also be used in pot-pourri. I'd rather keep walking on it in the garden – it's quite happy rooting down between paving stones in paths and patios.

## Clary (*Salvia sclarea*)

The true clary is a perennial which few people grow. Instead they plump for the arguably prettier annual, *Salvia horminum*, which isn't really clary at all and which used to be known as red-topped sage. It doesn't matter what you call it; grow it anyway. Scatter the seeds on to a patch of well-cultivated earth during spring and take them in. Thin out the resulting seedlings to leave one every 10cm (4in) and stand back and watch. The tall stems will grow up to 1m (3ft) or so and are clad in bright bracts of pink, white or purple which surround insignificant flowers. The blooms may come and go but the bracts last for most of the summer.

Many virtues have been ascribed to comfrey, but it is an acquired taste and perhaps best kept for garden use

Grow comfrey as a manure crop – the cut leaves placed on the compost heap will help other material to rot down. Wilted foliage is also supposed to increase potato yields when laid in the bottom of the planting trench.

## Comfrey (*Symphytum officinale*)

It used to be known as 'knitbone' when it was used as a cure for broken limbs; today it could be more accurately known as 'knitbrow' – introduced to a small garden its eradication becomes almost impossible. So be careful! The plain green kind is really of use only as a producer of green matter for the compost heap, but the variegated varieties are much less rampant and prized by keen gardeners.

Whichever type you plant, make sure it has a moist soil and a spot in dappled shade rather than full sun. It grows 60cm to 1m (2 to 3ft) tall and rather more across. Propagate by division of mature clumps in autumn or spring. The adventurous can make comfrey tea, but it is most definitely an acquired taste.

## Costmary (*Chrysanthemum balsamita*)

Alecost, or costmary, is not a plant that could be described as spectacular in any way, and yet it's a rather endearing thing to plant in the herb garden because its leaves are larger than those of most of its bedfellows. It will form a hefty clump, sending up stems to a height of

Costmary

Lovage was once used as a deodorant. Try a sachet in the bath.

Cotton lavender

1m (3ft) or so, and although the flowers are simply small yellow daisies, the grey-green leaves are saw-edged and aromatic.

The plant enjoys an ordinary soil and a sunny spot and is easily propagated by division in spring.

The youngest leaves have a minty tang and small quantities can be chopped up and added to soups and casseroles of chicken. At one time it was used to flavour ale, and the leaves, when crushed, are also said to relieve the pain of bee stings.

### Cotton lavender (*Santolina chamaecyparissus*)

Now here's a white-leaved garden favourite! You can call it lavender cotton or cotton lavender and either way it produces a mass of feathery foliage in light, bright grey which persists throughout the year. Crush the leaves and they release a rich and fruity aroma. It's a plant that can take quite heavy clipping, and indeed it's far better to be cruel to it if you want a dense and shapely plant. In midsummer, if you let it, it will produce custard-yellow bobble flowers like those of tansy. I'd rather clip it over with shears at that point and stop its fun – the heavy flowers simply pull the bush open so that it looks like a disintegrating pom-pon.

Plant new bushes in spring, and take cuttings from older plants in summer; they root easily in a propagating case. Plants usually grow 60cm (2ft) or so high when clipped, and rather more across, and they enjoy the poorest soil and full sun.

If you have moth problems in the wardrobe, try hanging sprigs of cotton lavender on your coathangers. If you decide to let the flowers develop, cut off the bunches as soon as they open and dry them for winter decorations. But I reckon cotton lavender looks best of all when it's clipped into a formal, flat-topped shape and surrounded by a lower hedge of box; very parterre!

## Curry plant (*Helichrysum angustifolium*)

Here's a herb that's even whiter than cotton lavender; its long, narrow leaves seem to shine silvery in the summer sun. It grows to a height of 45cm (1½ft) or so and even more across, and produces masses of small yellow button flowers in summer. Snip them off or leave them alone, depending on whether you value shapeliness more than colour (they tend to weigh down the stems).

In the coldest parts of the country the curry plant is doubtfully hardy but it will survive reasonable winters in the south. Cuttings can be rooted in a propagating case in summer and are best planted out the following spring.

The plant reeks of vindaloo when its leaves are crushed and it can be chopped up and used to impart its distinctive flavouring to a variety of dishes including scrambled eggs. Like cotton lavender it can also be used to repel moths and its flowers dried for winter arrangements.

## Hyssop (*Hyssopus officinalis*)

The only thing I knew about hyssop, before I grew it, was that biblical line: 'purge me with hyssop and I shall be clean.' Not the sort of thing likely to engender a feeling of goodwill toward any plant. But it's a real cracker. The leaves are small, evergreen, narrow and rather stiff, and the flowers of deep blue are carried in spikes during the summer. It makes a lowish hummock around 30cm (1ft) high and spreads sideways for twice that. As a border

Leaves of lemon-scented geraniums placed in the bottom of a cake tin will impart a delicious citrus aroma to a sponge cake.

edging it is excellent and can even be clipped into a neatish hedge. Try it and see.

It likes sun and a well-drained soil and is easy to grow from seed sown outdoors or under glass in spring. Cuttings with a heel can be taken from established plants at the same time. Garnish your salads with the flowers: the leaves are rather bitter and should be used with discretion in casseroles and the like. As with most herbs; if in doubt, bung it in the pot-pourri! Even if you decide to leave it alone in the garden, the bees will love it.

## Juniper (*Juniperus communis*)

I regularly recommended the horizontal-growing junipers for covering manhole covers until a plumber asked me if I'd ever tried to get down a manhole that was so concealed. It is a painful experience by all accounts. I've learned my lesson and will now recommend this one as an evergreen plant with frothy foliage that gives the garden a bit of body in winter. It's happy in most soils and situations and will eventually reach about 4m (12ft). The female plant produces the berries that are used in the kitchen so unless you plant a male as well you may be disappointed.

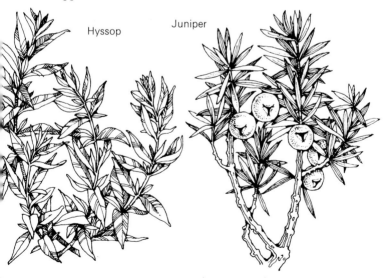

Hyssop

Juniper

Herbs are attacked by few pests and diseases but mint rust is particularly nasty. Dig up and burn any mint plants that show signs of orange spotting.

Propagation is by seed sown in a cold frame as soon as it is available, or by heel cuttings in a propagator in late summer.

If your plant does produce berries, you can use them in stuffing, in sausages and in marinades, and even in tea if the prospect cheers you.

## Lavender (*Lavandula* species and varieties)

No garden should be without lavender; it nearly always looks smart, it is deliciously fragrant with its own unique aroma, and bees love it.

There are many varieties to choose from, but of them all 'Hidcote' and 'Munstead' are, I think, the best. 'Hidcote Giant' is tall, up to 1m (3ft) or so with its flower spikes, and tends to topple, and the white and pink varieties tend to be something of a disappointment. The two varieties recommended are dwarf and only grow to 45cm (1½ft) or so. Propagate by taking cuttings in summer, and make sure you clip over the bushes after flowering to keep them tight and healthy. Unpruned bushes become straggly and short-lived.

The classic use for lavender flowers is in lavender bags, for which use they should be plucked and dried just before they open. They are also valuable (as if you hadn't guessed) in pot-pourri. The plant itself can be grown as an individual in a sunny spot in the border, but is at its most spectacular when used as an informal hedge, perhaps alongside a path in the herb garden.

## Lemon verbena (*Lippia citriodora*)

Easily the strongest-scented lemony plant in the garden; it beats lemon thyme and lemon balm hands down. Sadly, in all but the warmest countries, the plant tends to be killed off by the winter frosts, but where the winter is not too severe it will often spring up again from below ground level the following season.

It makes a bush up to 1m (3ft) or so high in a season, and where these shoots are not killed by the frosts they may eventually make 3m (10ft) or so – usually against a warm and sunny wall. The leaves are narrow and the tiny

Lavender, an essential element for every garden, neat in appearance and oh, so fragrant

sprays of white flowers rather insignificant – the scent is all! You'll have realised by now that the plant needs the sunniest and most well-drained spot in the garden, preferably against a south- or west-facing wall, and you'd do well to protect its roots with a thick mulch of straw or bracken or even sand come the autumn. Alternatively, grow it in a hefty pot that can be overwintered in a cool greenhouse.

Propagate it by taking shoot tip cuttings in summer. Its often recommended as one of the best lemon flavourings for puddings and it imparts a rich citrus fragrance to pot-pourri.

Grow your own pot-pourri border: plant it with old fashioned roses, lavender, artemisia, bergamot, chamomile, cotton lavender, hyssop, lemon verbena and mint.

## Marigold (*Calendula officinalis*)

It's the pot marigold rather than those charmless French or African types that's at home in the herb garden. Sow it once and it will be with you for season after season if you let it, for it scatters its seeds with abandon. The leaves are a fresh green and the flowers are many-rayed daisies of yellow or orange.

Lots of varieties are offered by seedsmen, but the really stocky 'Fiesta Gitana' types are so rounded of habit as to look rather artificial and lacking in grace. Avoid them if your taste is for the old-fashioned. Most grow to a height of between 30 and 60cm (1 and 2ft).

Sow the seeds outdoors where the plants are to flower in spring. They will die with the onset of autumn frosts. Give them a spot in well-drained soil and full sun.

The petals can be used to brighten up salads. Cutting off the opened flowers also encourages the plant to produce more, and if you don't want it to spread about this also prevents seed production.

## Nasturtium (*Tropaeolum majus*)

With its parasol-shaped leaves and its bright orange, red or yellow trumpet flowers the nasturtium is a cottage garden favourite, not least because it is so easy to grow from those pea-sized seeds that can be pushed straight into the ground where they are to flower by the most inexperienced fingers.

The climbing varieties look good when trained up tripods of canes or clusters of brushwood, and the trailers will sprawl anywhere in poor soil and sun.
'Cherry Rose' is an especially eye-catching variety with blooms of rich dusky rose.

A prompt spray with a systemic insecticide will bump off both blackfly and caterpillars which nibble at the foliage.

Garnish your salads with the flower petals and chop up the peppery-tasting leaves to mix with cottage cheese if you're a fan of unusual sandwich fillings. Seed heads and flower buds can be pickled and used in place of capers.

Beehives rubbed with balm are said to keep the bees at home.

Nasturtium flowers brighten up any salad and the leaves add piquancy to sandwiches

## Pennyroyal (*Mentha pulegium*)

Although it's really just a variety of mint, pennyroyal is often thought of as a distinct herb, partly because of its common name (which gives nothing away about its relations) and partly because it creeps flat along the ground, unlike many of its relations which rise to considerable heights.

There is, however, a form of pennyroyal which can

grow 30cm (1ft) or so high. The carpeter is better and can be used in sun or light shade to meander among paving stones or to make a small lawn. It has an extremely strong odour of peppermint and was at one time crushed and placed in beds to suffocate fleas!

Propagate the plant by division in spring, removing and replanting quite small rooted pieces. It is happy in sun or shade but does like to get its roots down where they can be cool.

## Rue (*Ruta graveolens*)

The plain-leaved rue is rarely grown today, thanks to the popularity of the blue-grey leaved 'Jackman's Blue', and a sought-after variegated variety. The blue one is the one to plant for best effect, but the plain species is dead easy to raise in quantity from seed sown in a pot in a cool greenhouse in spring. Propagate the other two by summer cuttings of shoot tips which root easily in a propagator.

Fennel

Rue

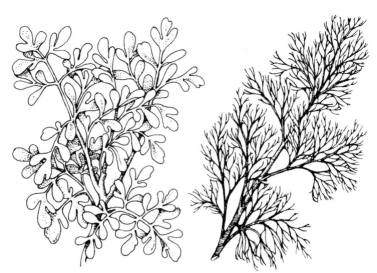

If you have difficulty in finding ground cover plants for shade, try pennyroyal and sweet woodruff; both will do well.

All have handsomely divided leaves and, if pinched out from time to time, make smart, rounded bushes up to 60cm (2ft) high and as much across.

The flowers are interesting, if not spectacular, being acid yellow with a green centre and carried in clusters during summer. Well drained soil and sun is all any rue needs to do well.

The crushed leaves are said to provide relief from bee stings if rubbed on to the affected area, but the stench is not exactly pleasing.

## Southernwood or Lad's Love (*Artemisia abrotanum*)

This is one of the most delightful grey foliage plants. Its leaves are amazingly fine and frothy and grow on stems that may reach 1m (3ft). I've never yet seen it flower, but then our summers are seldom competitive with those in its Mediterranean home. Give it a sunny and sheltered spot in well-drained soil.

Cuttings are easy to root in a propagating case in summer and the plant is all the better for being chopped down to ground level in spring and divided or replaced every few years when it becomes scrappy. It's used in pot-pourri and herb pillows when dried and is also recommended as a moth deterrent among clothes.

## Sweet Cicely (*Myrrhis odorata*)

In appearance, sweet cicely looks for all the world like a rather refined cow parsley. It's a perennial that's easy to raise from seed sown where the plants are to grow in spring, and mature clumps can be divided at the same time of year.

It will make a good 1.5m (5ft) and is one of those useful herbs that doesn't mind a moistish soil and a little shade where its feathery foliage and umbrella-spoke flowers can shelter from scorching sun.

The chopped leaves can be added to stewed fruit and fruit salads and the dried flowers to pot-pourri. Grow it for the evocative sound of its latin name if for nothing else.

---

Sprays of southernwood were often worn on lapels on a Sunday to prevent churchgoers from nodding off during the sermon.

The chopped-up leaves of sweet cicely can be added to most fruity desserts with success

## Tansy (*Tanacetum vulgare*)

I've almost reached the stage where I regret planting this herb because it is so invasive, but it does look delightful whether in leaf or flower. The form I grow is 'Crispum' with the fingered leaves even more divided to give them a ferny appearance. The custard-yellow button flowers appear in summer when the plant will have reached a height of 1m (3ft) or so.

Propagation is by division of the vigorous roots in autumn or spring, and the plant enjoys a spot in any soil and sun or light shade.

The young leaves were once frequently used to flavour tansy pudding.

## Woodruff (*Asperula odorata*)

The perennial sweet woodruff is a useful little ground cover plant for moistish soil and light shade, where it will carpet the earth with 15-cm (6-in) stems clothed in whorls of small, pointed leaves and topped with small, white flower clusters in summer. Propagate by dividing plants in spring.

Chervil seeds in vinegar were used by the Romans to cure hiccups. A cold key down the back seems infinitely preferable to me!

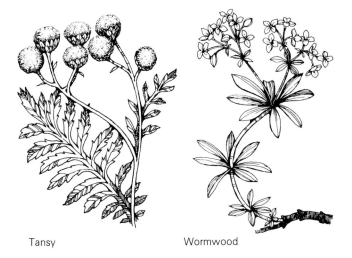

Tansy                    Wormwood

The herbal qualities of woodruff only become apparent when it is dried, preferably at flowering time – it smells of sweet, new-mown hay and was once used for strewing floors before the days of fitted carpets. Nowadays you're more likely to find it in a herb pillow or in pot-pourri, and a few sprays of it are a recommended addition to musty wardrobes and cupboards.

## Wormwood (*Artemisia absinthium*)

One of the most elegant of grey-foliage plants, wormwood is most usually grown in one of its most statuesque forms: 'Lambrook Silver'. The foliage has a lacy fineness and even manages to look reasonable in the winter months. The plant grows to about 60cm (2ft) and enjoys sun and a well-drained soil. Cut back the stems in spring to encourage new shoots.

It's recommended as a fly deterrent when sprays of foliage are hung up in rooms, and as a moth deterrent if they are hung in wardrobes. In the garden it looks delectable when used as a companion to blue or pink flowers or old-fashioned roses.

Propagate it by taking cuttings of shoot tips in early summer and rooting them in a propagating case.

## FRAGRANT DELIGHTS

The herbs that offer scent rather than flavour can be used in any number of ways to make your life more fragrant. With gardeners clamouring for greater perfume in their plots it is amazing that more of them do not try to bring these fragrances indoors, too.

### Pot-pourri

This is the name given to that flower petal and leafy mixture that scents the air so well in the shops that sell it and rather less so in the home. The reason for this is that the shop contains sackfuls of the stuff and most purchasers expect to reap the same bounty from a cupful. Be generous with yourself and revive your mixture from time to time with extra ingredients, essential oils or pot-pourri 'reviver' which boosts the aroma.

Some of the most delightful fragrances providing the ingredients for pot-pourri, and other soothing conceits

Dried basil leaves are used in snuff.

There are hundreds of recipes of varying complexity, but this one made from easily obtained ingredients will give you something to sigh over:

1 cupful of scented rose petals
1 cupful of lavender flowers
6 crushed bayleaves
1 cupful of lemon verbena, marjoram and thyme (mixed)
1 tablespoonful of orris root powder
1 teaspoonful of allspice
a few dried, crushed cloves.

All the ingredients must be dried. You can fiddle about with the quantities until you have a combination that is particularly suited to your olfactory senses!

## Herb pillows

Small, padded herb pillows 23cm (9in) or so square can be slid under your normal pillow to send you off to a scented sleep. The outer material can be chosen to suit your colour scheme, and an inner slip of fine cloth such as muslin can be stuffed with lavender, lemon verbena or sweet

woodruff. Cotton wool wadding pushed in at either side of the slip, before the outer case is sewn up, will give extra padding, but don't overdo it or the fragrance will find difficulty in escaping.

## Lavender bags and baskets

The flowerheads of lavender possess most fragrance just before they open, so remove them and dry them at that time. Pulled off the stems, the flowers on their own can be tied up in small squares of fabric to make the lavender bags that so frequently scent drawers and wardrobes, or the stalks can be retained and (while they are still green and pliable) tied together and woven with ribbon as shown in the drawing. Ten or a dozen stalks should give plenty of perfume.

To make lavender baskets, tie stems together, fold them back over the heads and weave in a length of satin ribbon

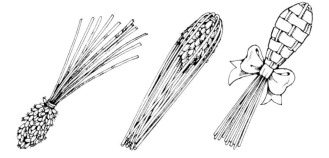

## Herbs in the bath

It's alright; you don't have to splash around in water that's covered in floating foliage. Choose your herbs, soak them in boiling water in a kitchen bowl and then strain the liquid into the bath. Alternatively tie a muslin bag that's filled with fragrant herbs to the hot tap so that the water runs through it. Fresh-smelling herbs and those with citrus fragrances are the most appealing. Some varieties of sage and thyme may leave you with the aroma of a Sunday roast. It's all a matter of taste!

Sprigs of the bay tree, *Laurus nobilis*, were originally used as the victor's laurel and can be seen around many an emperor's head on Roman coins.

# INDEX